THE WILL SAUNTERS
Pushing Onward

by

Zack Saunders

William "B.J." Saunders

Angela Mitchell

DORRANCE PUBLISHING CO
EST. 1920
PITTSBURGH, PENNSYLVANIA 15238

The contents of this work, including, but not limited to, the accuracy of events, people, and places depicted; opinions expressed; permission to use previously published materials included; and any advice given or actions advocated are solely the responsibility of the author, who assumes all liability for said work and indemnifies the publisher against any claims stemming from publication of the work.

All Rights Reserved
Copyright © 2020 by Zack Saunders

No part of this book may be reproduced or transmitted, downloaded, distributed, reverse engineered, or stored in or introduced into any information storage and retrieval system, in any form or by any means, including photocopying and recording, whether electronic or mechanical, now known or hereinafter invented without permission in writing from the publisher.

Dorrance Publishing Co
585 Alpha Drive
Suite 103
Pittsburgh, PA 15238
Visit our website at www.dorrancebookstore.com

ISBN: 978-1-6491-3510-0
eISBN: 978-1-6491-3927-6

The Will Saunters

Pushing Onward

Part One:

Angela Mitchell

Prologue

(11/22/2013)

Angela R. Mitchell

TIME IS OF THE ESSENCE. The essence of what? Time is all we are given in this life and yet we spend it frivolously as if it's a never-ending waterfall. The currents carry and take us through all that we endeavor. Then one day even the current flows no more. The water dissipates and eventually there is no longer a trace of its existence. We are told that there is another life after this journey and we must die from this world in order to be rebirthed into the new.

Everything is a result of lessons learned and decisions made. Yet we tend to repeat behaviors until some life-altering event occurs changing the path of which takes us to our destiny. I cannot fathom what lies in the next dimension, but know there must be something there.

Loved ones gone are waiting for us to join them. I feel there must be life after this one because even though I can no longer physically look loved ones in the face, I feel their presence around me. It's not something that can be explained, it's a knowing.

I imagine a world where words aren't needed. Pain and suffering, longing for those gone from us will be no more. I often wonder what they are doing at this very moment where time isn't measured by a clock. Eternity seems so far away, but yet I reach my hand out knowing that one day it will be my turn to be rebirthed.

My cries reverberate out into the infinite and I can only hope they reach the one I send them out to. It's so hard to be connected and then have the chain that binds lose a link. Love never breaks. It holds on by the tiniest thread if need be and never gives up. Time must be the essence of that… Love.

Time is the essence of love. It is the one thing our existence and purpose was built on. It grows and branches out but never loses its roots. No one can steal that from you. You have to give it up freely in order to lose it. Even then, its roots are so embedded inside you, it's impossible to break its grip.

Even as a child is sprouted from a mother's womb, so are we from our Creator. We either grew with or away from him, who allows even me to sit and write down these words on this paper. However, we are never uprooted from the Love that started this life as we knew it. No matter how much we try to fight what is inevitable. We must remember… Love will prevail in its time.

Silent screams fill her head

Unexpected wishes for her death

Love long gone

Nothing more to carry on

Her scattered heart shattered into more pieces

She swallows words she shan't say

So her tears mean all the more on his brightest day

Screaming Silence

Hush

Tears roll down her face as he speaks the words she never wanted to hear

He holds her heart in one hand and his conscience in the other

Doing what he knows was the best thing to do

Even though Love started this, it somehow was lost in the mix

Deceit, betrayal, and emotions have control now

Some things….Love can't withstand

It fills her pain and allows forgiveness and time to take their toll

Time ticks on….

Runaway

The voice inside my head screams

He's all better now

No need for you any longer

Still a convenience

Hold down the fort while he's away

Uninvited in his world

Constantly bidding his time

None of which is for me

If just once in a while

Being a family could be his #1

Another call on the phone

He has to run

Sorry, you can't come

An inconvenience for him

Too busy, has things to do

Run away, run away, run away now

He'll never miss you

My Children

I look at you and see a Love I've never known

Believing that it's something that will not change

No one can take you from me

I'm whose womb you came from

Even though you don't understand everything that happens in life

Know that I'll always be the light that brightens your way

Without you, I'm nobody

I need you as much as you need me

It's you who makes me whole

Little things you do, tells me that it's the same for you

Hold on tight and don't lose faith in what we can do together

Otherwise, we're all lost

I am truly blessed to have all of you in my life

Rest assured that I'm always on your side

Scared Child

Where is the one who sang me a lullaby?

She's gone somewhere, don't know why.

Where did she go? Where could she be?

I need her here holding me.

Follow Me

Take my hand and follow me

I'll take you places you never imagined

Experience with me the true meaning of life

For no one can surely live life to its fullest alone

With you I'll share my world

Together we can have it all

Apart all we can share are dreams of how things could be

Daydream

Once in a daydream I shared my life with you

Once in a daydream my wish had come true

Once in a fantasy you held me tight

Once in a fantasy I loved you with all my might

It feels like an eternity since I saw your face

Love Songs

The thought of you with someone else tears my heart in…two

I thought you'd be in my arms forever and I'd be loving you

Now my arms are empty and you are gone for good

Our paths forked their separate ways, destined to never cross again

You were the light of my life and meant the world to me

Now our worlds revolve around a special one who will always be the best part of us

Looking into his eyes I see a light burning deep

Only then do I know…it's worth it all

Although things are for the best, I'm missing part of me

Moments in time I'll always hold dear

It took until now for me to hold my head up and be free

Still…a part of me longs to change the face of time

Hearts can only be deceived so many times before explosion

Still…every song reminds me of you

I'm singing Love Songs in the cold

Where this road leads I just don't know

This force pushes me along

Finally realizing all the things I did wrong

Hold Me

Somewhere in that faraway stare,

I know deep within is someone who cares.

Just by the little things you do,

Makes me realize the one I Love is you.

It's not so much the things you say,

It's how you show me in your own way.

I'm scared sometimes that I'm falling too deep,

I pray that I'm the one you keep.

Hold me close to your heart,

For there, is where, I'll never part.

Thinking of You

A few days have passed, but thoughts of you are impressioned in my mind.

We need to work a few things out,

Still, there is always time.

You have wild oats to sew,

I also need time to grow.

Never forget the one that's still our bind,

The core of our Love that's hard to find.

Although we have grown apart,

You will always have my heart.

Knowing You

I never imagined that one day you'd be in my arms and I'd be Loving you.

I was just a face you had seen in a crowd.

You were a stranger yet, always around.

Another person, who one day, would disappear from me.

Still, here you are, with me every day.

My only regret is that I never had the chance to know you sooner.

Every night I go to sleep holding you in my arms.

Nothing has ever given me greater joy.

Feel

The days drag by and the nights seem too cold

I can almost feel you by my side

I imagine your touch and feel your breath against my face as you kiss me goodnight

Dreams of you…

dreams with you…

Still feel real to me

Don't Let Go

You touch me like no one ever has before

Crossing a bridge I felt had long been destroyed

A sweet reward I find myself longing for

You carry the key to my soul, unraveling me until I can no longer hide

Opening doors that I had forgotten existed

Stirring up feelings I thought I'd never feel again

Yet, here I am for your taking

Don't let go

Don't Turn Away

Don't turn away…for the tears are falling slowly down my face.

Don't turn away…for my heart is breaking with each step you take.

Life's mysteries seem like a faded dream.

Nothing good in life is ever what it seems.

I wish I had the word to describe,

this lonely feeling I have deep inside.

All I know is without you I'm lost,

a broken heart is my cost.

Don't turn away

Us

As I look into your eyes

I struggle for the words to say

Losing myself in your heartbreaking stare

Searching for answers of how things got this way

My days are empty and the nights too cold

Inside your arms is where I long to be

Hoping every day that you'll come back to me

A losing battle that pushes me every day

I've given you wings now so fly away

I pray in life, you'll be everything you ever wanted to be

Once the last feather of your wings is gone

Know our son will carry us on

The road seems too rocky, no solid ground in sight

At the end of our journey is Love's pure light

I'll lock our memories deep in my heart

For that is all I have left of us

The Love I Gave

I walk by you now hoping you'll look up at me

Our Love was something you just couldn't see

I waited and waited for some kind of sign

There was nothing there for me to find

I know there's Love and kindness in your heart

I thought I felt it from the start

The security in your arms, the warmth of your touch

Why did you say I Love you so much

Right from the start 'til the very end

My heart I cannot mend

In rough and troubled times I held you close

But where were you when I needed you most

You act like you don't care

I know you remember a Love we once shared

You wave a slight hello and goodbye

One thing's for sure, you'll never see me cry

Though the days may be long and the nights grow cold

You'll never again have me to hold

You'll never find a Love more sweet or kind

I guess you don't know what Love you left behind

As I walk by you now trying to be brave

I ask of you one thing

Remember always the Love I gave

Past

I can't seem to erase you from my mind

Your memories haunt me as the pain cuts deeper each time into my soul

Showing no mercy as I cry out for your Love

You're so far away but I can still feel you by my side

Only now you're merely a mirage teasing my heart

All I have with you now is a past

You can never take that away

Hardest Thing in Life

One of the hardest things in life is standing back and watching a Loved one leave you behind. An emptiness fills your gut because part of you has been ripped away. The loneliness takes its toll and you see no reason to move on anymore. You reach out to grab the Love you lost, but find nothing because the sea of destruction has drifted them too far away.

Worth It All

Watching the rain beat against the window

Thinking of the times we've shared

Seems like a lifetime ago when it was me for whom you cared

Now there's an infinite distance between us

A stretch that I cannot conquer but need you to meet me halfway

Our days are numbered until our little one arrives

A day that should be blessed for he is part of us both

A bond that just might make the bad times seem…

worth it all

Haunting Me

Crying to the stars

Carrying this pain in my heart

I search for the feelings I felt from the start

Those happy days have long since passed

Nothing good in life ever seems to last

I miss those melodies that you used to sing

To this day I still wear your ring

I no longer can hold you close

Still your memories haunt me the most

My Heart

Flow with me through the sands of time

Together we'll see things untold

I'll share with you my secrets of life

Let's see what we can find

Here is my heart…

Do what you will

Just be gentle and hold it dear

Buried deep is a treasure of Love

Look under the heartache and scars from the past

Cover it with kindness and a tender kiss

Give time a chance to heal all wounds

Replace them with memories of everything we do

Hold me tight, for I'm afraid too

Pull me close if I start to slip away

Tell me of the things you feel inside

Untold Stories

Driving down the street, I saw a man walking along. He seemed strange to me. From his dirty blue jeans to his torn flannel shirt, I wondered if he was a traveler. If his shoes could tell me the places they've walked. The sights they've seen. I wish I could hear the stories of the hand fate has dealt for him. If he had children, did they know of his existence or did he know the joy of having them? It's funny how we can look at someone else and automatically have an opinion of them without knowing the untold story behind them.

Rainbow

I see my rainbow slowly disappearing taking away my pot of gold.
If I were the sun I could shine brighter to bring back its rays.
But then, I can't shine forever and my rainbow will surly diminish away.
Then all I have is the memory of my beautiful rainbow.
I nourish it within me.
As long as I keep it alive, then I will always have my pot of gold.
Our relationship is the rainbow and my Love is the sun nourishing it.
What we have between us, what we work for, what we share…
Is my pot of gold.

◉

Shattered and battered

Eternally scarred

Choices made got me this far

Longing for yesterday, I sit and I wait

As if somehow it will change the hate

Paths that I picked were rocky and hard

I just pray that they lead me to where you are

◉

Your words are vibrations echoing through eternity's infinite space.

Ricocheting off the walls in my head, slicing through my heart and soul.

Like a double-edged sword leaving me scars that I can't seem to heal.

Time cannot mend the brokenness I've become, but I know…

Warriors can't fight battles they aren't trained for.

When my head becomes silent…

Then I'll worry

Her Light

She beams her light through the darkest days
Reaching out into the unknown
Holding to the hope he will find his way
Treading the path she knows won't last
She steadies her feet all the same
Yesterday slips through her grasp
Tomorrow still too far to reach
As years pass she carries her grief
In silence as she weeps
Beaming her light through the darkest days
Until her body finally gave

◉

My words fall onto deaf ears
My feelings are disregarded
Let my silence feed the tears
From Hope's Port, Love has departed
Keep all of you yesteryears
Be back where you started
Too crowded for me in here
Once again I'm brokenhearted

I Stand Alone

I stand alone in this big world with my big heart to pick up friends

when they need lifted.

When my job is done, they go on their merry way and once again

I stand alone

I swallow fear and hurdle obstacles that some coward from…

coming out a stronger person and yet

I stand alone

The foundation on which I stand shakes beneath my feet, but still I cannot falter.

On me, is all of whom I can depend, to cross the finish line in this race called Life.

All of this I do alone and

I am victorious

I give all that is asked and then some

Still I stand alone

The foundation again trembles beneath my firm feet

Still I stand alone

The storms rage trying to shake me

Still I stand alone

To withstand isn't enough, I must survive

As I stand alone

The sun will shine tomorrow and dry the wreckage

And I stand victorious

In the Still

I sit quietly in the still

feeling his breath upon my neck

I sit quietly in the still

feeling his arms around my waist

I sit quietly in the still

hearing his rhythmic heartbeat

I sit quietly in the still

embracing his presence guarding me

In my moment, all is as it was

until the still moves

I'm left alone to carry on

searching for another quiet moment

in the still

◉

The downfall of making good memories is…

you can't relive them physically

After all the drugs and alcohol are gone…

all you're left with is yourself

No one is here to hold you and say it's gonna be okay…

Okay is what it won't be again

I close my eyes and recollections fade into my head

Filling it with times and experiences during my journey so far,

So wanting to hold you again

Good Times

◉

The best rose in the garden you plucked for your bouquet had the one thorn. Each time you prick your finger, you instantly cover it with your lips and suck your own nectar. Trying to preserve all of yourself that you can. Each speck that drops takes away that much of you. Such creatures of habit, we still reach for that rose again to hold as we admire its beauty. Life's cycle completes and its beauty corrodes. Leaving behind a trail of scars from its thorn, where it pierced and left its mark. Grateful for its memorable time.

Bittersweet

Sunshine

I hope for a dream

dream for hope

Wondering which will be the first to come

The dream seems a bit cloudy

Hope is fading a bit

Maybe the dream and hope stirs together

That would explain the mist

For it wets my face

In my dark days

Will the sun ever shine?

My strength has grown weak

No longer helping me stand tall

Courage seems a bit out of reach

Both gone without reason

Deteriorated in times passing

Darkness chills my heart and soul

Chaos swirls my mind

All that's left is nothing

I feel so cold

Will the sun ever shine?

The sun filters its rays through the sky's layers, shining its welcome warmth through her

window of opportunity. If she could only keep her eyes fixed on its light, she might find her way

through the lonely darkness consuming her aura, trying to dim her light within. She holds her focus

with all that she's made of and is inspired to get up once more.

Unrecognized

I long for how we used to be

When you were you and I was me

Gripping hard to memories

The Love there is bittersweet

Mirror, mirror, who do I see?

This shattered girl, who is she?

Days drag on and life moves along

Leaving me drenched of its lessons

Drowning in experience

Expressing all of my wisdom

Living in my memories today

So I may have them tomorrow

Beautiful

The brightest star on the shiniest night is where you'll find me

Shimmering amongst the Angels, I'll forever be

Dancing in the Heavens, my binds gone, I'm free

I'm not too far away, just look up and see

I'm the whisper in your ear and the wind kissing your cheek

The pain inside your heart is how much you mean to me

Time spent together now will be shared inside our dreams

Call out and I will hear the Love you send to me

For now we say goodbye

Love you forever and eternity

I am always yours

Teressa Lee

The Pond

The shallow pond lies quietly by the serene grassy knoll. Basking in the reflection of the Lovers, who trespass there, unleashing their unbridled passions. Its waters ripple their moment in time, just as it has for the ones before them. Encompassing their memory inside its pit along with the tears of the clouds. It masks their secret rendezvous within the sky's silhouette, telling only the ones who come back to reminisce in their escapade and makes them smile once again.

Empty spaces filled with words unspoken

Replaced by times we have shared

Impacting each other's lives

Changed by lessons learned, never to be the same

Although our time has come to travel different roads

Doesn't mean our time well spent together ends at the fork

We must gather our stones and take them with us on our journey

No matter how heavy the load

Grateful for our golden friendship

I've had the pleasure of making your acquaintance

No matter how long the distance or time we spend apart

You will always be with me

Hand in hand, heart to heart

Thank you for the opportunity of knowing you

We can never move forward without growing at home

Home is where the heart resides

More

No more words can I speak with you in front of me

No more memories without this anguish I breathe

No more seeing your smiling face making my day

No more decisions to make to help find your way

No more laughter to fill this empty space

No more hugs and kisses to help know my place

No more tears of sadness or even joy

No more good times to rid me of this void

No more working your day away

No more relaxing or watching your children play

So much more taken from our lives that day

So much more you had to give for us to enjoy

So much more of you in this little girl and boy

So much more of you is now my fantasy

So much more left behind in your legacy

So much more I'll always miss

So much more to add and subtract from our list

So much more than most will ever be

So much more missing from the soul inside of me

I take what you left me and always wish for

More

With silent tears she purged her soul

Held in pain, she finally let go

Each word from his lips pierced her heart

She knew it would from the start

Still, benefit of doubt she gave

But Love was never made

It shattered before her eyes

With each and every lie

One day she found no pieces of heart left

Over memories she continuously wept

It wasn't because she didn't care

Reasons of pain she could no longer bear

You can't refill a heart

That's ripped and torn apart

Too many trespasses there

So many scars to wear

Silent tears fall from her eyes

She lived so many lives

History kept repeating itself

Lessons leaving behind their whelp

Her shattered heart turned to dust

Due to words she couldn't trust

With her soul to light her way

Her silent tears are her November rain

Cleansing what now feels like her cold, heartless soul

She clings to its light for that's all she does know, to be true

Part Two:

William "B.J." Saunders

Introduction
The Longest Thoughts

I've had the longest thoughts about these…

Words that mean

something to be heard

should have a sound

of their own

Instead we gather here

at the tip of mute tongue

beneath the smile

of a light

that's turned off

The struggle of the walls

strain to hold up the world

listening

I sit here alone

whispering what I'm told

to the stale air of a night

with a breeze that refuses to move

I Practice the Art

The color of her presence

the sound of her hair

under the influence of the soft morning breeze

the shrewish glimmer of her stare

hardened

by the clock's unwinding

The absence of language

in an empty bed

across her tongue

the faint smell of her dreams

The distance between Love and her heart

the honesty of anger

the place she'd rather be

Through silence

I practice the art

A Liar

When violets were blue

if I told them the truth

they'd know I was a liar

Where I've Grown

Colors change

to the shape of a page

and dreams go

where they know

Some people blossom

and fly away

Some lie there

unnoticed

Some hearts beat

to the change of the day

Some beat

to leave it alone

A scribbled name

at the top of a page

or the bottom

of where I've grown

The Sully of Her Dream

I walk away from a day

oh, she's mad

alone with herself

nothing missing

I bury a bone by a stream

nothing bad

I tell myself

all in good intention

I toss a stone into a pond

by a tree growing

along a day

When nothing would sing

I spend time alone

to find myself missing

against my will

and the sully of her dream

In Tune

Time, days,

and a girl I used to know

remind me of a bottle

in the next room

Shadows from sounds

of the trains going by

whisper reasons

to a new moon

People in colors

of songs with no name

Or the distance

from me to you

Stay scattered across

the pages of my mind

randomly precise

and in tune

Lost for Words

I sit in circles

inside my head

side by side

around the curves

Unshapely and broken

patterns reveal

through my decay

lack of concern

True words of wisdom

I once read

change color and shape

as they blur

Time with all its patience

quietly stares

as I sit here alone

lost for words

Piece of Heart

Sometimes days

end in a way

when the sky sounds empty

through the telephone

an alarming glare

from a see-through face

a clock that knows the time

and the way home

Something afraid

behind some courageous

or the purchased rings

never worn

never enough time

to reveal the ageless

piece of heart that protects

the soul

Saved for Truth

Dream aloud
goes to my head
lost and found
misunderstood
damaged proud
staggering friend
not as down
as you are good
lonely crowd
bastard end
beds in aisles
plastic mood
happy houses
secretly binge
boxes of smiles
saved for truth

Truth's Own Wing

Nights on days

piled to the sky

take time to hear the sermon

of a trickling brook

moments of reasons

years gone by

washed by the currents

need to sing

lights on the hillside

darkness' eyes

cover to cover

know the book

the changing of seasons

reasons to lie

set flight on truth's

own wing

Fools of Love's War

Off, on

responsive to the touch

sleep alone

should have known as much

all along

painted like rust

the flower that blossoms

to hide the thorn;

In, out

lost in such luck

sit along the edge

anticipate the push

fist clenched

full of lies and Love

never knowing enough

to expect any more

just live and die

fools of Love's war

Fracture Bones

Days found on doorsteps

horrid Autumn mornings

breath tilted in silent whisper

tolerated pain

Shallow puddles accompanied

along alone to her

a secret place

Dirty hands

splashed clean with lies

crawl like worms

across the page

Tired words

see-through eyes

fractured bones arranged

on a broken plate

Another Missing Sparkle

Words coagulate

at the tip of my tongue

too slow

to scatter themselves

through time

thoughts go dancing

even though still young

attaching themselves

to my life

She lives where she is

without understanding

the difference between

hers and mine

Another uphill

to keep me standing

another missing sparkle

in my eye

Beside You in Our Room

The way my mind sways

against things I believe

the way my heart staggers

'cross thoughts

across my day

the way my feathers ruffle

when it's time for me to leave

my reflection stained

in a child's ball of snow

no reason we can't get along

that he should know

the night

the day

and several weeks before

lie blistered and labeled

truth untold

terrified

we sleep alone

our names the same

you before I

beside you

thought beside thought

though apart

the same

never wishing the end

to collect its dues

I'll be here

the same as before

alone

beside you

in our room

Her Phone Call

I spoke with an Angel

who remembered my name

her voice fastened

my life to her heart

such simple words

her velvet tone

or the thoughts of

she used to be mine

What a dark day

I'm running out of time

she needs to know

how I felt

or at least in my mind

it didn't always hurt

and her phone call

rendered me well

Candle without a Flame

The biggest part of my life

when I was alive

was with you…

remember that?

I remember making Love

until our hearts exploded

and then holding you

as close as I could

to what was left of me

in silence…

do you remember that?

As far as I know

I'm standing in line

from the back to the front

or from the side

the way I grow

Or misunderstanding

how ships sail astray

against the tide

how far I go

along for the ride

Or the people who remind me

of my pain

thinking they know

the meaning of demanding

Or the time it takes

for one more day

To violate time

I exist

it seems

omission's to fault

influence Jim's beam

insulated by thought

transpiring quaint ideas

regulation

procedure

dominance

or truth

no longer appear

on the backdrop

I use

She calls my name

in a dream out loud

my dream

or hers

or both

the distant rumble

of the approaching train

reminds me of how

we were close

She sleeps behind the walls

in the corner of my mind

through a window

where the sky frowns

she crawls beneath the floor

or up and down my spine

by a candle whose flame

is blown out

Used to Make Her Proud

Through a piece of glass

she whispers a scream

with all her nerve

enough to turn the lights down

She knows my color

and what I mean

and she feels secure

where she's at now

My hands change numbers

with each pendulum swing

cautiously watching

the world go around

The air that I breathe

and the time that I need

belong only to the way

I used to make her proud

What We Can Write About

Pieces that don't fit

get left behind

words

ignored

aged

in my ear

Feelings that scar

never healed

spend costly time

in my life

Liquor doors

sore

exhaustingly

swing open

to replenish

the dry spells

caused by time

If time determines names

then people turn into things

that we can no longer

write about

Chance, Tolerance, and Luck

We came out at night

We didn't meet

We just melted

But she knows what I mean

And I know she can feel it

I guess that's why we live in dreams

Nothing makes sense

neither does this

but in a way

it's easily read

Broken bottle bits

empty bottle fits

in a home like this

understood

Days without skin

months clothed in glances

traded through a mirror's

soapy scum

A year without a kiss

two nights in a row

with

the balance of chance

tolerance

and luck

Rancid Patterns

Fastened by chains
to the silent majority
obligation binds
the gears of my soul
Interchangeable feelings
flattened on edge
blunt their way
through the stone
Extensive consideration
of impassive conflict
a ridiculed child's
broken bone
Rancid patterns
of rusty links display
another young heart
grown old

Memories of Yesterday

The heat from the tower

drags down along the fields

the color of their hearts

long, black and grey

The emptiness in their lives

forever filled

with hiding under shelves

piled with shame

Corners full of meaning

hide their faces

until lamplight decays

into day

Beneath a broken stone

their shadows lie

along with memories

of yesterday

Find the Way Home

We can all be found

grouped in connecting

spaces

But like water

shallowness

levels its way

back down

empty eyes

with full hearts

of empty choices

or empty hearts

with eyes full of Love

dumped out

Away I'm secure

with this ridicule

in close

I'm nailed to the floor

trying to understand

this region of error

prying myself loose

I let go

on the edge

of complications

hard breath sings

words of soft

misfortunate tone

to scream or sleep

beside a vacant mind's

struggle

and take time to find the way home

Done Wrong

Another fight with you

just out of habit

another broken window

nobody's fault

one single afternoon

without static

One more drink of wine

to make me fall

all we've been through

so pathetic

The only thing to show

are broken hearts

All I know to do

is sit and regret

every little thing

I've done wrong

Life's Decay

Teeth rounded
to life's decay
portrait forbidden
time lost for play
Sunlight flowering
in shades of grey
outlined smiling
in brilliant stone
Memories
of each moment
that paved
the road

Take Some Time

Flushed out

like water through a ditch

my time with you

has been drained

torn out

like flesh without a stitch

Memories of you

scar my mind

blown out

like a candle without a wish

Worn out

darkness overcomes the flame

unused

like a broken dish

I guess

this is gonna take some time

Just Another Day

Passion

arrests itself

at your doorstep

Through the keyhole

bitter feelings escape

The walls' ears

have sewn themselves

shut

Emotions

and reasons to change

attachment

to potential disasters

in stride

The stressed link

that broke the chain

rattle the cages

of the criminal inside

Disturbingly yet

just another day

Strangers on Another Page

Words I say

cradle attention

utterance

surpassing themselves away

Caressing the point

with aggravation

displaying the crack

in the pane

Even tide sunsets

flawed by imperfection

remember as we lie awake

Regretful yet passionate

feelings exchanged

with strangers

on another page

In My Head

You taker, you triumph

You conductor of violence

You soft-spoken reason

You tread

You Lover, you hater

You composer of silence

You answer to questions

misread

You link to complication

You obtainer of strength

You monster

with people like hands

You teacher, you student

You abductor of balance

Why do you live in my head?

Passion

Shadows

corners

and darkness thereof

seeing myself to play

Considering the value

of locked passages

time's bitter out

these days

And the passion that grows

melts beside me

an icy patch

I've engraved

It crawls through the corners of my heart

and gnaws

at its hollow shape

Random Issue

Political crisis

a child starving for information

murder routinely announced

old news

Pointless conversations

in particular battles lost

resistance impairs

feelings I use

Charred nourishment

essence of survival

intoxicated

on a bottle of youth

Inconclusive thoughts

not concerned enough to care

on a layout

of random issue

Last Winter's Skin

She speaks my name

in wooden tongue

Suspicious of her feet in soil

flowering thorns

In the sun's red clotting

fruitless

heartless

and cold

Wooden framed walls

like her fingers all around me

Rusty nails

twisted boards

lie buried in leaves

Last winter's skin

we've tangled roots

I know

Reflection of Me

The cost of what it takes

to make the world go around

the value of being

without me

The time it takes to make

another sun go down

the reason she cries

in her sleep

The day's gone missing

without a piano's sound

another song my voice

just couldn't sing

Another sunny day

with its heart torn out

Another reflection

in the mirror

of me

Condemned by Love

I feel like a man

clothed with no skin

everything I touch hurts

Or the thought of them knowing

what I really am

I've been condemned to death

by Love

Try Again

Happy endings are just stories

that haven't been finished yet

In the end you start to think

about where it all began

If I wanted you to stay

we'd still be in Love

And although it's over

I still have this ring

There's no more air to breathe

around you anymore

And if no one loses

then no one really wins

So let's both stand tall

and call this one a draw

And tomorrow on my own

I'll try again

Gold in the Hills

It's a long trip

up that river

above

Some try

to get more than their

fill

It's easy to drown

In a river

without Love

But if you make it

there's gold in those

hills

This Ride

She crawls on her back

and kills with her heart

She left with the part

that understands time

An hourglass exhausted

with no use for sand

Another misspelled word

underlined

Tears in my pocket

as cold as I am

No longer have a reason

to try

Spinning in a world

as old as I am

I'm ready to get off

this ride

Your Love

I'm coming undone

my hands are too cold

to hold it in

All of the colors have gone from my eyes

as black and white

as where I've been

I was born into a world

in which nothing fits

As vacant as a cemetery

full of lost souls

Questioning answers

simply dismissed

I once had a life

but at a great cost

I'm so close to the end

I can smell its breath

In what's left of a world

that I consider lost

Why do new beginnings

always seem like the end?

Why does your Love hurt

the most?

Your Shame

Do you know

which colors I'm not?

Can you hear the songs

I can't sing?

Can you feel what I can't

in the middle of a night

with silence too loud

to dream?

May your shame be painful

may your pain weigh you down

May your weight

feel as helpless as I did

It's a shame

but I'm over you now

May your shame be graceful

May your greed

burn you somehow

May your burns be grateful

grateful that you're doing

without

May your dreams be wasteful

May all your waste

gather in piles

stacked to the sky

May your shame

haunt you now

Need to Fly

She lies silently

in tall grass

as mysterious as the sea's abyss

Downwind and curious

cautiously waiting

with prudent policy

in her eyes

Frozen in a time

with declination to pass

as confident as a mountain peak

kissing the sky

Warning nor shame

could hold her back

another reason for

needing

to fly

Intention vs. Decision

Friendly fire?

Contradictions and

reasonless meanings

Or maybe something

she already knew

The wind whispers

as the cars go by

The whistle of

a songbird flew

Nevertheless

because of the mess

The distance in time

that we do

Cause a feeling

of lost emotion

Separating what I mean

from what I choose

Broken Footsteps

The broken clock…

fair winds

and flowing seas

Stop the clock

so time won't know

Blind the mirror's

reflective eyes

With the purest of linen

cover the bones

Creased faces line the aisles

row by row

See-through places

hide the grueling miles

Of broken footsteps

dusted in snow

Comes Out Wrong

You know that I can only say these things

when I'm feeling better

And I know that you know

that won't last long

And with all this noise in my head

these words tangle and clutter

So forgive me if this comes out all wrong...

Lost Seasons

I saw a ripple in the moon

through a hole in the sky

where the shape of its sound

fell through

At the corner of a sound

dancing on the breeze

A lost emotion

found its way

It's been a thousand years

since last summer left me

Too many seasons lost

to relate

Love Getting in the Way

Exchanged glances

that we both pretend not to see

just Love getting in the way

Exhausting nights

with each other in our dreams

just Love getting in the way

The perfect song

with words too cold to sing

still Love keeps getting in the way

Worn-out memories

of the way things used to be

yeah,

it's just Love getting in the way

Crooked Lines

They were imitating angels

and hanging from their wings

They lost their lives dancing between pages

to songs with no words

blaming each other for crooked lines

Rainy Day

I'd never take you down this far
you'd never last that long anyway
you belong in a frame
a picture of your name
with both hands on your heart
on a rainy day

Your Heart without Me

When days became years
I became alone
and light became the only thing
I couldn't see
your eyes became tears
I could hear through the phone
and your heart, without me
skipped a beat

One More Yesterday

Time's getting cold now
The air's growing old and I
Feel you lookin' at me that way
So I'll pretend to be strong
and move myself along
looking back will only make me
want to stay
I know you're tripped up on words
It's O.K. You're just a girl
and I think I know what you're
trying to say
So close your eyes
for the rest of the ride
I'm pretty sure I know the way
and as I'm running out of time
feeling my heart die
there's only one thing I'd like to say
Thank you for one more yesterday

Lost Name

Tongue too tied up to scream

out of my mind,

he's loose from his cage

boned too deep to bleed

out of time

I've lost my name

The Nerve to Be Okay

When days fall down

and doors are closed

I pictured you

through a windowpane

I remember the sound

of a breeze that's blown

Or the color of your eyes

that the skies stain

The shape of your voice

when it made me cry

And the time it took

to get through the day

Your sorrowed look

when we say goodbye

And the nerve it takes

to be O.K.

Have to Cry

If I never live without you

at least you'll know I died

If I never again say I love you

at least you'll know I tried

If I never again dream beside you

I'll never again need to lie

If never again my thoughts wonder upon you

never again will I have to cry

Where I Walk Away

You wrote the lines, you changed the time to every beat I played

You drank the wine, you moved the signs that keep it safe

I grew up knowing that it'd always be this way

You changed my mind, time after time

This is the part where I walk away

Every Side of Me

All that you are
and everything you need
tears a hole
in every side of me
The distance of your heart
every time you leave
leaves room to grow
on every side of me

Pulled My Voice Gone

These songs in my mind
have pulled my voice gone

All That Remains

Your voice didn't hurt me today

I put your memory in the shadow

of a passing train

no longer mine

You're down the line

He can have all of your pain

You can take your show

on the road

draw the curtains

Let me go home

All that remains

separates the grain

on a hillside's

blanket of snow

this time I _have_ to let go

Reasons You Still Haunt My Mind

I have answers

for all the questions

I have reasons

for all the lost time

I have emotions

that still miss you

There are reasons you still

haunt my mind

Death's Dignity

Death has a dignity

all of its own

Don't be so proud

you're not the only one

Now Found

As the wind pushes the wires

the flags struggle to free themselves from their poles

Time patiently turns my direction

through the sunshine I can see the air blow

People too scared to be around me

find their hiding places where they all go

For so long I was lost but now I found me

it's just a shame I'm the only one who knows

Deep Down Inside

Every time I fly

the sky don't seem as blue

as the color of your eyes

like it used to

Every time I die

it's 'cause you wanted me to

Every time I cry

I'm thinking of you

Every time I try

it seems that there's no use

to understand the reasons

why I feel the way I do

'Cause deep down inside

lies the only truth

that every time I cry

I'm crying over you

Changed Heart

What made you change your heart?

Spinning Record

The record is spinning again

…but we're not on the song we want to be.

But I Am

The moon's not full this time

but my mind is

And I can see a pattern forming

off layout

The reasons not this time

but I am

Learn the Truth

The more I try, I find
I'm steadily reminded
of the time that divides
the truth, through me and you
The more I try to wind
the clock that holds the time
the time that fills the clock
learns the truth

This Monster's Friend

Monsters I love, that look like me.
Feed themselves when they can.
Drink by drink, too dizzy to see,
This monster holds my hand.
People I shove, scared to leave,
Give me all that they can.
In hopes to one day, obtain my trust,
And be this monster's friend.

Feeling This Way

I miss your laugh

the magical things

you say

I miss your lies

and the way they

go away

I miss coming back

and never wanting

to stay

Guess I miss every

part about

it all

But I don't miss

feeling this

way

Can't Make It Work Anymore

I'll take my chances

on the edge of the road

long, distant glances

the years before

misunderstanding

pretending to know

something there always

worked before,

it's time to take

my show on the road

blown out to sea

like a stone

the sky spinning by

dimly ignored

severed from requirement

hardly known

the distance of our hearts

spiritually close

but I can't make it work

anymore

Inspire Me

So random and free,

the wind embraces you,

lifting you by your wings

full of your own life,

seemingly to share,

you choose my windowsill

to sing.

Tones so brilliant,

with each sharp chirp,

describing your flight

like a dream.

A few crumbs of bread,

the peace of mind,

you'll be back to inspire me.

Distance from Me to You

Under a wicked moon

the only thing that moves

the time that the clock holds still

and the distance from me to you

Spreads My Wings

A never talk today
just another tired of listening
from yesterday
another walk away
a reason that's missin'
never too far gone
a never see the way
another understanding
why things fall apart
another walk to stay
too tired to miss the way
you bite to the bone
seem to be the only things
that spread my wings to fly

Exact Smile

Her smile is as exact as
the silver line around a star

Bottle I Trust

My thoughts press deeper into my glass

almost worshipping the results

The world I'm leaving twists behind me

the one I love fills my soul

The world I need now denies me

my works of glass appear all broke

But this bottle I trust feels the faith inside

my mind so level its marbles won't roll

Architect of Her Misfortune

I am the architect of her misfortune

People in Your Life

Do I dance in your mind

like you do in mine

when you're away

do you dream of me in circles

or shades of red?

All the people in your life

that make me wait in line

make me crazy

at least that's what I heard

from a voice in my head

Third Dimensions

Third dimensions

honest lies and

loving hearts

lonely dances

lonely eyes so lovely

scared

lightning flashes

last three times

a broken heart

only dances

only times left in the dark

Slice without a Scare

A slice without a scare

that everyone can see

with nowhere to go

or nowhere left to be

Perceived Fiction

Sometimes it seems

it's just make believe

and the other times

it's just you and me

and I think I want it all

Lady Winter

I grew up with a wind

as lazy as summer

She always knew my name

except when Lady Winter

would hold me down.

Time Won't Wait

Just like a dream that never got away

I woke up from a long time ago

But who understands dreams anyway?

The thing is time won't wait, the dreams get… old

Can't Escape

You're stuck here now in this song
You can't go away

Been This Far

Things come apart
and you were scattered
in the road
I've been this far
left of center before

Understood

One time ago I talked to a wise man
He told me everything I'll ever need
is gonna be in the smile
of the girl I'm gonna learn to love.
When I see you smile
I know what he means.

My Thoughts

Walk along a while just for a daze

Tell ya about my thoughts

and the way they go

and see if any of our stories

are the same

'cause there can't be much to life that you don't know.

Come Back Home

Come on back, baby

Don't know where in the world you went

Come on back, baby

Don't know what in the world I did

Said come on back home

baby, if you ever get tired of lovin' him.

Lost the Truth

I no longer can see
so I just stare.
I remember when I lost it.
I just can't remember where.
I'm still lookin' for pure feelings
or reasons that still care,
but somewhere in the glare
I've lost the truth…
the fracture that split our
hearts in two.

Creature of Habit

Underline what you meant to say
Borderline gonna take it away
Never mind if U R afraid
You're a creature of habit now

Double Check

Everything is frat and away from the edge...

It's almost like I don't have to double check anymore

Silent Beauty

If we are always guided by other people's thoughts...

what is the point of having our own?

She walks in silent beauty like the night

burning out this fuse up here alone

Front Row

We sit in the front row because we want to be the first ones to see it

Be You

It's all on me, to find the words

that make it all seem O.K., it's all on me

The time I waste hiding in my cage, don't follow me

don't make the same

mistakes

And if I leave before you bleed

just know one thing

it was always me

who wanted it to be just the same as everybody else but…

time didn't agree

Don't follow me

Just be yourself

Disorderly Presence

I exist here

in no particular order

just to make you smaller

with words

Never Too Late

Where do ya think you're gonna go?
'Cause girl, I know ya and I know ya know
How big the world can be
When you're all alone
Yeah, and I bet it's a long and winding road
Yeah, and when you get there I want you to know
If it's too cold
It's never too late to come back home

Guilt Train

Don't count the days,
go down the road
like a photograph of
a guilt train

Unraveled World

The world unraveled on me at daybreak. I have to be strong. I must cope with this fallow void in my life. My disposition to my alarm, my depthless approach, is merely an act. Obliquely my comprehension of it all blurs. To seize a smirk from the mirror in routine is repugnant. It would seem as if there were a grudge. A cup of coffee to restore my mind, fractured from last night's unsymmetrical dreams. Cure the blindness of the windows. Try to figure out what it is that's gonna hold me together today. And begin to manipulate the morning.

What happens to all those dreams? And love? What happened to love? I sued to feel that I had a pretty good understanding about life. Here lately I just don't know. Maybe it was love. Maybe that's all the better it gets, and I was expecting too much.

I wonder if she feels the same. She has to feel a sense of freedom that she never had when I kept her locked in this cage. Just that alone is enough for me to justify the thrill. I miss having someone around to talk to, God knows I love to talk. But I don't miss all the arguing and hard feelings that seemed to occupy damn near every minute of every day there at the end. Looking back now, I know I could have avoided a lot of that. I'm just too fuckin' bullheaded.

Zachery is the main reason. I think we've put that poor child through enough. It's a shame that we're making him witness our stubbornness. It's making him grow up too fast. He will find out that the world isn't the magical playland that he thinks it is soon enough. I hear him playing in the next room, and he is so far away from all this depressing confusion. That gives me a sense of security. I need to play with him more than I do. It's just hard to get my head out of the clouds. Well, thanks for listening.

So it's just me and my thoughts again. Hooray! I guess this is where it all really happens. Solitude. No, better than that self-inflicted solitude. I don't really know what it is about being alone that keeps me tight in its clutches, assuring me that if nothing else, it will always be there for me. Waiting until I make my way through another useless relationship, neglecting, and abusing any and everything I can, almost as if I were trying to find my way back to it. Maybe it's the freedom. Not having to please anyone but myself. That couldn't be that hard. Could it? I often wonder if it will always be this way.

A plant doesn't have eyes. No way of seeing which direction the light really comes from. But yet it reaches in the right direction somehow, getting stronger and more sensitive to the light all the while. I wish love was like that. I wish I could just sense which way to grow for the best nourishment. Once I discovered the source I would get stronger and stronger, until I flourished into a relationship of endless unconditional love. OR maybe some pointless sweaty sex with a total stranger would be the best thing right now. It's hard to make tough choices when there is no one around to help you see every angle. That's probably why I've made as many mistakes as I have. But most of those mistakes have produced something good before going ass backwards. And that's what's brought me to where I am today. Alone.

I think if I had the choice to do it all over again I would have to pass. I sure have a lot of regrets, but I think they make me who I am. My life's etched in stone. And I feel like it does me good to be able to look back at the things I've done wrong, but also things I've done right groove their way through that same piece of stone. And it helps to revise them too.

Well, as confused about everything as I am right now, I'll look back on this paper someday and laugh at my petty little problems. Hopefully things won't be worse, but I'm sure they'll seem more complex. And I'll wonder why I was always such a crybaby. But until then, or until I find someone to share my life with, I should say, I'll be here alone.

Very Much Like Me

When she's afraid to be near me

she's a lot like I am

Cover My Trades

Like a machine that chews things to pieces, you don't care if I cry or scream while you do your business, you just do your business. Tooth after tooth spitting pieces out into a bloody pile, the only sound you hear is the hum of your own motor turning your gears. Maybe caught up in your own thoughts, never thinking of what's happening to me. At least, that's what I think it would be like if you caught up to me, so I keep sinning, never looking back. I still imagine the sound of your appetite hungry for me and my dreams. It keeps me on my toes. Always covering my trades.

Tomorrow?

A day without a drink. A face without a smile. A heart with no beat. A moment that lasts a while. The kind of day that makes you wonder what it is that determines the way things are gonna be. As time unfolds itself into a pile of events exhausted, my mind examines each instant carefully. Not one microscopic speck is to be overlooked. I need to figure out what makes it all go. I need to know that if I had to I could keep myself together. All the pieces. Not falling down as I always have in the past; wallowing around in my own self-pity. It was there behind the wagon where I met some of my so-called best friends. But now I can see. My vision has finally straightened. A good buddy stopped by today, drunk. His nonsense drove me nuts, but I wasn't rude. It sure was an eye opener. I know I acted just like that when I was drinking, but then it didn't seem like it. I always thought I acted cool or levelheaded, but how could that be? Everyone else acts like a fool and I, the cool one, behaves as if I were a Jekyll and Hyde monster who gets himself back to normal by drinking this antidote: alcohol. Yeah, right. Anyway, I feel a sense of accomplishment at the end of the day when I do make it through it sober, and unbelievably okay…

I wanted a drink so bad earlier and I knew that just one wouldn't be enough. It never is. Or was. Sometimes it's hard to find something to take my mind off that ever-so-popular chemical that they have formulated to taste so good. But I've redirected my desires before and didn't die so I know I can do it when I need to, like it or not. God knows I've been under the influence and probably came within inches of death on several occasions, but for some strange reason still survived. Just being able to realize that should be enough to keep me sober. But still the urge is there. Like Satan himself, tempting me. Go ahead, just one never hurt. Hell, have a couple. Remember how good they make you feel? Don't you need a break from all the bullshit you deal with all day? The worry, the stress, the pressure that other people put on you when their lives are falling to pieces and they can't find a way to keep it all together so they take it out on you? Don't you think a good stiff shot will help? Go ahead, medicate yourself. Tend to the way this fucked-up world leaves you feeling. You'll behave. You always do. Remember?

But then eventually it passes. It doesn't fade, just all of a sudden I know that a drink would be the doom of me. And something about being sober makes me feel alive. It makes me aware that the world has been spinning for a long time and I've been too dizzy to notice. Just pissing it all away.

I am fully aware that I have to face tomorrow heads up, and nothing is gonna change other than the changes I decide to make. I am stuck with this condition that a sober person would call a habit, or maybe even call me a drunk. Which I really don't mind, because I know it's all up to me and my choices.

Today, no drinks.

Tomorrow?

I'm Done

After a lifetime or as a few days seem so close

that look in her eye that turned away

a tear in her eye

and a lump in her throat

remember why I want to stay

Sad thing no one will know

I'm done

Not to Know

Don't you ever think that the days would be better if we spent more time to-
gether than alone?

Don't you think I'd love you better

If you didn't leave me on the doorstep in the cold?

Sometimes I sit and think

Does the whole world feel the sunshine come and go?

Sometimes I sit and drink

Guess it's easier for me not to know.

Off-On

Off-on

responsive to the touch

sleep alone

should have known as much

all along

painted like rust

the flower that blossoms

to hide the thorn;

in out

lost in such luck

sit along the edge

anticipate the push

fists clenched

full of lies and love

never knowing enough

to expect any

more

just live and die

fools of love's

war.

Seized Requital

To seize one's

transcending requital

unwieldy

soiled in guilt

confined by curbstones

love's detest

credible

to immature regret;

one's obsessive reproach

intrusively pundit

must catalog

each denouncing step

to perceive assessment

of impending value

detaining only

self-abasing

descent.

Left Turn

Turn left, at the edge

of your mind,

it's a shortcut to the

next page

down past the dreams

or what you wanted me

to be:

a broken window to view

the day

if there's anything left

to believe

under dead skin or fallen

leaves

it's certain to shine

the other way

Holds My Heart

Taking chances
all my life couldn't fool your heart
Question answers
learn our way up through the stars
Lightning dances
across the sky, that's where we are
Taking chances
stealing time back from the clock

But that's the way

she lives to love me

when she leaves me

And that's the way

she loves to leave me

in the dark

And that's the way

I need to be here

when she needs me

That's the way

she holds my heart

Passing glances

second time is who you are

Second chances

across my mind a second scar

Lightning dances
across my life and through my heart
Second chances
second place is no place to start

But that's the way
she lives to love me
when she leaves me
And that's the way
she loves to leave me
in the dark
And that's the way
I need to be here
when she needs me
That's the way
she holds my heart

Cosmetic Decay

Cosmetic decay

copulates a bottle opener

reliance falters

florid display

cheval glass

realm of composure

re-proven altered

besotted survey

feelings come amiss

culvert's daughter

surfeit passage

counsel outlay

neutral tint engaged

cathedral ceiling

mirror's imagination

reflecting on

each day

All Still Here

Storm clouds

rolling up around you.

You left a lot of us here.

Don't remember a day without you,

and now you've disappeared.

There are times life swells over the little things

that keep most of us afloat,

and there are too many times

we don't get to say goodbye,

when it's time to go.

I know everybody here knows you,

and I think you know that they know.

If things could be different

they would be,

but this time

you're on your own.

It's impossible for us here to share a smile,

single file, up and down the road.

We need you to know.

As far as you've gone,

we're *all* still here,

and you're *not* alone.

Goodbye (Again)

Ya know they keep me here deep inside

peering through those eyes.

They say it's why I'm still alive

They're better with my head.

Ya know I always tried

to get back to the surface

fight my way outside

just to realize

I'm just in time to say goodbye again.

Ya know I like it on the edge of me

where my skin can feel the sun

reaching through this darkness

free from all I've done

crawling up the stairs backwards

looking for the one

who's sleeping in the next room

dreaming of being done.

And I'm just in time to say goodbye again.

Time Clutches Dissolve

I don't have every piece of me anymore
the blade's edgeless slander shaped me like the wind
He breathes too much or they were too hard to listen
The silence it takes to grow a boneless grin
Now wait until time clutches dissolve
above the room whose passage stakes claim
to broadcast fragments determined by law
absent or scattered down a rainy day

Got It Made

Nothin' up my sleeves
my bag's always full of tricks
I got it
hard on the words
easy on the mix
I got it
Everything I need
so much it barely fits
I got it
A world that always turns,
a head that never quits
I got it hard
I got it made

What I'm Having

Rarely want what I'm needing

Rarely go without

Boy, let me tell ya when I'm needing

What I'm wanting

It's what I'm having now

Already There

And I got my problems

And I got my ways of dealing with it

And you got your options

Go away or help me get through this

Some of the strangest days of my life

They take away from this dog that needs to be fed.

And the closer I get to the bones I buried

You're already there.

Evaluated Distance

If you look at your reflection at the bottom of the well

what you see is only the surface

If you try to see the meaning hidden underneath

the measure of the depth can be deceiving

The bottom has a rocky reputation

you can feel it in the distance

the deeper down you stare

From up above it's hard to see

but you'll know it when you're there

On the bottom words are shallow

on the surface talk is cheap

You can only judge the distance

by the company

in the eyes of the confessor

Sit and Wait

So I sit and wait

for this nothing to come

to see it on my skin

to dance with along alone

All Wrong

It's all wrong, it's my fault, it's been so long,

since you told me why,

daylight comes, to wake alone, friendly tones,

find a place to hid,

same old song, bottle strong, found a hole,

keep it all inside,

etched in stone, dragged along, broken home,

empty sky,

never shown, branded bone, lost and cold,

never try,

healing slow, room to grow, life to go,

one more time.

If You'd Answer the Phone

I walked beside the dreams you left
When I realized that's what you meant
When you told me you were going home.

We never seem to sing side by side
And no wonder it never came to mind.
I'm scared to let it show.

I'm sorry about the things I said
And I'm sorry if I made you feel
Like I'm the only one.

Walking alone I found the time
To let the things you said
Turn into a smile
And I want to let you know—

I feel so far away from last night
And I wonder how to make it right
And if you're even home…
And if you'd answer your phone…

In dreams I keep, the time I bide
It's not so far from the heart you hide
Just chews closer to the bone

Sometimes I see in this make believe

The other side of what's you and me

And I want to take it home

I feel so far away from last night

And I wonder how to make it right

And if you're even home…

And if you'd answer your phone…

Hole in Your Smile

Nicks and chips

and pieces missing

they're counting holes in your file

man, you're all tangled

up in the wire

Nicks and chips

and reasons missing

chasing drinks for

your smile

you keep your problems

all so neat

in a pile

and to hear you play

they'd say

the world's turning

for you

and the life you're

learning to live

is starting to learn

your tune

and I hear you say

someday

you're gonna make

it through

if you're ever gonna

fly

boy, you better find it

soon

Nicks and chips

people listen

to the holes in

your life

and the air feels

so cold on your

wounds

all the broken sticks

and magic tricks

you got your hat

full of lies

and you're starting

to make them come

true

oh, the price you pay

to change your shade

from grey to blue

and the life you learned to live

has finally learned

your tune

and I hear you say

there are days

you never made it

through

if you're never gonna

die

man, you better find

it soon

Nicks and chips

and pieces missing

there's a hole

in your smile…

3rd Dominions

Third dominions

3 more times a broken heart

good intentions

3 more times 3 X the hurt

Story of My Life

I know what she'll say
and it won't be fresh linen
And the songs we'll never sing
essence of my time.

To fall from such a place
as high as we've been living
And piss it all away
the story of my life.

The time it takes to waste
the years that we've been given
Share thoughts of better days
in the middle of my mind.

My dreams yesterday,
gone not worth rebuilding
Crawl beneath the sheets
in the corner of my eye.

Hard times can take down
even the toughest fool
Hard times can teach the truth
to lie
Hard times can make you want to

walk away with yourself

But she knows the story of my life.

They used to go away

but something here she's different.

She took it all this way

and sleeps right by my side.

So it seems this way

with nothing real to give her

Let her keep her smile today

tomorrow make her cry

The story of my life.

Find My Way

And I'm feelin' weak

stolen from all the courage

I need

I bleed from my mind

when you're not around

Gotta find my way out of

the dark somehow

Protein for the Mind

Protein

for the mind that wastes away

and for words that sound like the noise in my head

which,

by the way

under a blanket with

the soft rumble of your life

in tune,

they seem like words I'd

want to know

and the time I miss while

you're away

Don't Follow Me

Don't follow me this way

there are pigs in the river

find the long way but follow it home!

Don't Need My Touch

She knows he's weak…

and hides from me.

Confined in her fortress of solitude,

she'll be safe.

They'll not speak again on this day,

I'll do his bidding.

Against his will he watches her fade from the room,

and his life.

He loves her,

I don't.

She's ragged,

wretched,

and inconsiderate of humane feelings.

She leaves him in the dark,

alone,

always,

expecting only that he meet her standards.

That's good.

It's not their problem,

it's mine…

ours.

She lets me know.

She don't know I'm struggling with my life.

Nobody does!

To get upset,

but now I just try to make sense of it.

I've ruined her day off.

She gets her frail feelings hurt,

she comes to me to cry about it.

Got all those people she surrounds herself with to comfort her.

But when she's "good,"

no mistaking that!

Don't need my touch anymore.

Part Three:

Zack Saunders

Rough Transition

I just can't stand this position I'm in

God, please help me transition again

At home I'm alone, surrounded by sin

Got sins of my own; why do I abound judgment?

This is a cry for help. God, I call on your name

Astounding and lame, surrounded by shame

I feel alone and helpless, bounded by chains

God, I need help accepting the change

I know I'm not a slave, 'cause through you I've been saved

Thank you, God, for showing me your love, mercy, and grace

Through these hard times, I know that I'll grow

Time shall fly by; I still have hope

Thank you for being there as closer than a friend

And for forgiving me, once again

Numbing Pain's Hope

They portrayed the portal to Painless Now
    and I was everyone else
        in fictitious heaven.
Suppressing that which was meant to be dealt with.
    procrastination.
Joy turned to numbed scars
    until it all fell away and they became opened gashes.
        ruined.
The hopefulness of forgetting via lung destruction
    until reality hits harder
        after time flies
            when it was supposed to be rewound.
True pain is feeling
    after contentment that isn't.
By God's grace, healing came
    when rushed no more.

Unnoticed

I used to believe you were in no condition to be a dad.

I felt like I had no father. But it didn't hurt *this* bad. Dag…

I feel like God made a mistake when he made me.

I can't pretend to be okay when I feel like the world hates me.

Once again, I'm going through another heartbreak.

Guess I gave her my heart, same rookie mistake.

Sometimes I think there was nothin' different about it

But there is—this time you're not around for me to talk about it!

Got tears streaming down my cheek over idiotic stuff

As if mournin' your death isn't problem enough.

It hurts. And that we can't talk only makes it hurt worse.

I'm goin' insane in solitude while my anger only spurts!

How can I love, when I can't even love myself?

I hope you're in heaven. I've had enough of this life myself.

I can't stand to feel. I almost don't even blame you for drinking.

I am my own worst enemy when I sit alone, thinking.

Does <u>anybody</u> notice?

Enduring

The world
>   strips me bare
>   and proceeds to shake me violently
>   while spinning at a million miles an hour
>   not caring to know my mind
>   my past
>   death
>   does it enough.

God, I'm afraid.
>   I fear.
Vulnerability.
>   Hurts.
Reminders why I'm not alone
>   because I can't be.
The only reason
>   I choose to feel
>   is because you remind me
>   it's best.

Tears
>   that show
>   this wasn't the original intention.
Pain
>   reminds
>   thorns weren't here
>   to stick in our hands
>   in the beginning.

Love

    endures

        and foreshadows

            hope, joy, and peace.

the way it was meant to be.

Pursuit versus Done

Thunk… thunk-thunk-thunk… thunk…
The familiar sound of memories.
Thunk… thunk-thunk-thunk… thunk…
What once was romance with butterflies
     is now a stab in the shattered heart.

Thunk… thunk-thunk-thunk… thunk…
The mulch, the glass,
     clanging together
        in one last attempt
          of reliving—
            or rewriting—
              the past.
Thunk… thunk-thunk-thunk… thunk…
Tears pushing their way past her eyes and down her cheeks,
     she remains seated on her bed,
        back against the wall
          to the right of her window.

Thunk… thunk-thunk-thunk… thunk…
Wishing it was only bugs in the winter,
     she pulls her legs up to her chest
        and cradles
          in the fetal position,
            waiting for the heartbreak outside of her window
           to let her be
             as if she could sleep.

Thunk… thunk-thunk-thunk… thunk…

"I'm sorry," streams her angelically broken whisper

    as she covers her ears

        feigning strength long enough to endure the moment,

           wanting with all her heart

             to alleviate his pain

                and subside her own.

Thunk…

The final toss of mulch at the window,

    followed by peace

        —concluded with painfully silent goodbyes, as he now under-
        stands it's time to move on.

Bitterness Comes

Bitterness comes to me.

Derived from the freshest wounds, the fork-tongued liar slips into my sights

with his slithering sidekicks

Aggravation and Temptation,

murmuring low and high enough to spark some curiosity.

Forgetting how full of poison these serpents are,

I bend low enough to listen

long enough to pay attention

and become sucked in by the cause of division

forgettin'

last time I fell for this

I was bitten.

Bitterness comes to me.

And for some strange reason, I pay attention.

God, please help me not to listen.

Not to Turn Around

Heading my own way,

    taking the best route I know home

    and it's taking every fiber of my being

        not to turn this car around.

We said some unkind words,

    not the way I wanted it to go,

    and it's taking every bit of my strength

        not to turn this car around.

The harder we tried,

    the more it took its toll on you,

        and that's a sharp reminder

Not to turn this car around.

Sitting at home,

    shedding the tears of a healing boy,

    I know I made the right choice not to turn around.

No longer crying 'cause my shattered heart

    but because of how far I've come,

    I did the right thing not to turn around.

I miss you like crazy,

    as goofy as it may seem,

    but I'm glad I didn't turn around.

Whatever will work out will work out

    whether or not I want the next results to come about.

I know God helped me not to turn around.

When you're off in college

  and I'm moving on in life,

  will it even matter then?

When you get a house of your own

  and I discover later strives,

  will it even matter then?

By the time you have a husband

  that hopefully treats you better,

  will it even hurt me then?

By the time I get old

  and I remember the beauty God once let me behold,

  will I still want to see your face again?

Teenage Boy

The teenage boy

    with slight mutton chops

        sits in his thinking chair,

            storing abundant passion,

                hoping to share it with the world

                    through his bluish eyes

                        and his endearing presence

            filled with consuming love—

                ecstatic about finding what to do with it next.

But for now,

    he will remain seated,

        fixing his compassionate eyes

            on the matching gaze

                of the precious, fragile, pearly eyed, black-and-white cat

                watching through the glass door

                    serving as the necessary prevention

                    of their yearning embrace

                    so as to prevent

                        an unnecessary indoor flea
                        infestation.

Never Forget Jim Beam

He put his hands on her.
    It hurts.
        I tried to forget.
Rough words that lead to violence.
    Destructive speech turned physical.
        It hurts.
            I tried to forget.
Scenes of parents arguing
    brings the buried back to surface;
        the tears of anger return.
        It hurts.
            I tried to forget.
Pouring out the bottle
    turned us broke
        to replace it.
        It hurts.
            I tried to forget.

I tried to forgive Jim Beam
    after the peace he stole from us
        and the artistic blessing of a life he robbed from us
        to shove into a casket.
    It hurts.
    I'll never forget.

But I know God will turn the garbage to flowers
    if we let him.

Hope Later

You sit in study hall, gettin' sick to your stomach.

Swarms of poison butterflies, and you're supposed to love it.

The cost of the price to pay just isn't part of your budget.

The consequences are *real,* but parts of you crave to bluff it.

They're callin' you to fish like you were trained to do.

The conflict of what feels like wisdom and flesh are strainin' you.

These hopeful feelings aren't for you, you wonder why they came to you.

After the last four tries and fails, it just ain't a game to you.

Where do you go from here? Do you just sit and wait?

Until the time passes and by then it's too late?

Or do you follow your dreams and do what you contemplate

Until you fall deep and drown in the cause of later heartbreak?

The system wasn't set up for you to hold on.

You might be ecstatic, but then it's time to *move on!*

Plus your prior knowledge, reminders to let it go for college

Maybe Dad was right, there are no happy endings…

Until tomorrow.

Poorly Constructed Walls

Can you see the passion in me?

Or do I have thick walls?

I forget they're not glass

and they're too unstable not to fall.

I was placed on this crooked floor.

I don't know any more

than to nail my walls to these crooked boards

with <u>tape</u>.

I crave so bad to let you in,

but I've been trained.

The closer I let you get,

the more I push you away

and for logical reasons.

Unless I desire to live in anxiety.

Growing up with cute sharp-toothed dogs,

I've been bitten in this society.

All I ever wanted was to scratch on their bellies,

but that was too bold.

Their ruthless actions showed.

Now I've got four sets of teeth marks

calloused and scarred

on my tender arms

and a slushy heart,

waiting for me to knock down the walls

and let some heat in.

But if I do that,

    you'll become another brick

        and another worthy cause

            for the frantic construction of my tall walls.

            I bet'cha.

Vulnerability?

To prematurely miss someone

    is a clear implication of the danger zone.

Is it better to take the risk

    or to continue on alone?

To let someone into your unstable heart

    requires your permission to rip it out.

Due to previous experience,

    it seems the emotional thought of another

      is only sweet

        until poisonous.

Innocent Thieves

How do you protect the heart on your sleeve

when you live amongst thieves?

They ALL seem innocent.

They <u>ALL</u> seem different.

But, "in the end, it doesn't even matter.[1]"

Screw it.

I've got eternal life

here and now.

What can mere females do to me?

"In the end,

it doesn't even matter.[2]"

---

1. CBS Interactive Inc., "Linkin Park - In The End Lyrics," MetroLyrics, 2020, *https://www.metrolyrics.com/in-the-end-lyrics-linkin-park.html).*

2. Ibid.

Nightmare of Reality (for Now)

It's a stalemate struggle to be at peace
  when left alone
    to overthink
      when the protagonist thoughts that brought genuine joy
        and good dreams
          become the antagonistic thoughts
            that cause inflexible anxiety
              when you wake up
                to the nightmare
                  of your new reality.

But God'll get you through it
  and you'll grow
    as usual,
      and you can choose
        to inscribe positive words
          to properly conclude negative perceptions
            so as to desperately cling
              to the hopeful truth,
                even when your lagging heart
                  won't let you feel it.

Situational depression
  will go away
    and feel better
      when it quits hurting.

Persevere,

because it's only gonna suck for now.

Serene Memories

Shedding fresh tears in an accompanying Bible

before heading into desired tranquility

on a sunny trampoline

immersing myself

in the making of magnificent memories

with the one who never leaves me.

I come before him with matter-less heartaches

compared to destitute others

and he offers me bounteous hope

through what sticks out to me most.

Still hurts,

but it could be worse.

These words

serve

as a steady release

of overbearing anxiety

while God cleans me up.

I praise God

for the blank pages he provides

in the treatment of this disease

titled "cold heart."

'Cause This Hurts

Nightmares of being shot, and Dad can't hold me in his arms

'Cause Jim Beam took him from me and now he's gone.

Hopefully over time, I'll learn to quit trustin' women.

The sugar-coatin' looks so sweet, but underneath you meet the venom in 'em.

Every time I try to heal, I screw up and let 'em bite me.

They <u>ALL</u> seemed like they liked me…

I just want someone to hold me and show me

That I'm okay, and maybe take the time to know me.

I'm broken, and I'm about to fall apart

If I throw me together alone 'cause on my own this is all too hard.

Missin' the companionship of a female

Until she rips my heart out of its socket because we failed—

Just to take the pain out for a minute. I'm tired of bein' in it.

If I don't share my load, I'll be cemented in it.

But I'm afraid to share my pain, wantin' no one else to feel it

So I turn to writin' rhymes. Hope God'll use this to heal it

'Cause this hurts..!

D.I.L.G.

Sparklingly beautiful blue eyes, centered with sunshine yellow

Flashy and luxurious hair

A well-proportioned nose

Attractively oval ears

Pretty teeth

A contagiously warm smile

Tinge of a noticeable overbite

Eyebrows—placed on too artistically for tweezing.

Dag! I look good :D

Mutual Scars

A charming lawn with prosperous trees.

Freshly mowed grass and a spot for a trampoline

to play on,

and maybe lay on

to watch the ceaselessly transfiguring clouds of daylight

or the pivoting stars at night.

A wonderful house to call it our home.

Perfectly spacious to play hide-and-seek

with gas-powered heat,

functioning plumbing and electricity

room for five queen-sized beds

and a full-house family,

and that's including the upstairs!

Something's missing.

And you can only tell

if you've been told

or have been next door

during desperate wails for help

that never came.

We are lacking two parents who love each other

enough to maybe get along

and God on the governing throne

that James Beam was invited to claim,

and Jimmy's a baseborn bastard.

Now I sit here on the rotting porch,

nearly grown,

admiring the consistency of nature's beauty

from the perspective of the lifeless house

now inherently mine,

mourning the innocent suicide

of a father with pure intentions

and that which was lost

and damned

from the conception of the first one-night stand:

<u>a happy home</u>.

So I take what I didn't have

and provide it for the little girl

with similar blue eyes.

Innocent,

yet worse off and more calloused than mine.

She needs me.

She needs God.

And I plan to show him to her.

For it takes the courageous heart

of a wounded soldier

to comprehend the pain

of a processing amputation.

Secured in the Familiarly Unknown

Secure in the unknown,

I care not what happens next,

so long as my every step is calculated

in the light of wisdom.

Each day I fear the LORD

whether Yahweh is the true pronunciation

or it is okay to render him as the LORD,

I know not,

but I know Christ,

and therefore I know my God

personally.

Jesus has got me now,

so I'm Jesus-gotten.

No male or female can strip that truth from me;

so I am free to rest in the hope of salvation

and sanctification

unconditionally,

even when it seems I'm on the verge of falling

and completely shattering

into megapixel-sized pieces.

Until further notice,

I will continue to worship my God

through it all.

What Can I Offer?

Would say that I don't have much,

but the truth is I've got a heart full of hope for whoever's in need of it.

Sometimes I'll throw it out there with a chance to get it trampled on.

Might hurt me for a little, but it's alright. I'll keep trampin' on

with the hope that I keep clampin' onto.

You can tug it till I'm cramping in my thoracic area

But it ain't moving. I'm not budging. I'll get hurt, but I've got more than a
passion for it.

The Unfamiliar

I'm secure in the unfamiliar. It's getting familiar to me.

Reality's been upside down for so long, it's getting realer for me.

If what I hope in isn't real, then how come I've never been triller

Than the lever of trill I feel even in the suffocation of what actuality's
dumping on me?

I'm learning how to make my pillow out of dirt

On this concrete slab, learning how to deal with hurt

Clinging to my god, the only access I have on how to have genuine mirth

While writhing in the joy of the fact that situations can't take out the amount
that I'm worth.

I'll be honest with you, I've been feeling lonely lately.

Call me homesick, I'm sick of this home; I've been craving my home, lately.

Surrounded by God and people, yet my soul still feels like I'm on my own
lately.

Still craving a girl to be a part of my world rather than chasing every carrot
I'm shown,

but maybe…

The tears keep coming. It's feeling real now.

But not real enough to let them flow out. I can't even feel them trying to *come out!*

No sense in writhing in self-pity. I've still got my God right here with me.

He's already overcome, and one day, I'll be living in *his* city.

References

CBS Interactive Inc. "Linkin Park - In The End Lyrics." MetroLyrics, 2020. *https://www.metrolyrics.com/in-the-end-lyrics-linkin-park.html.*

www.ingramcontent.com/pod-product-compliance
Lightning Source LLC
Chambersburg PA
CBHW061518050726

47593CB00002B/623